DATE DUE

APR 2 5 2006			
MAY 2 8 2013			

Profiles of the Presidents

FRANKLIN PIERCE

★ ★ ★

Profiles of the Presidents

FRANKLIN PIERCE

by Barbara A. Somervill

Content Adviser: Harry Rubenstein, Curator of Political History Collections, National Museum of American History, Smithsonian Institution
Reading Adviser: Dr. Linda D. Labbo, Department of Reading Education, College of Education, The University of Georgia

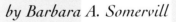
COMPASS POINT BOOKS ✧ MINNEAPOLIS, MINNESOTA

Compass Point Books
3722 West 50th Street, #115
Minneapolis, MN 55410

Visit Compass Point Books on the Internet at *www.compasspointbooks.com*
or e-mail your request to *custserv@compasspointbooks.com*

Photographs ©: Hulton/Archive by Getty Images, cover, 3, 8, 9, 14, 15, 17, 24 (bottom), 26, 27 (top), 33, 36 (top), 39, 47, 49, 54 (right), 56 (left), 57 (right), 59 (right); Stock Montage, 6, 23, 25 (all), 27 (bottom), 38, 44, 47, 54 (left), 58 (left); North Wind Picture Archives, 7, 11, 12, 18, 20, 21, 24 (top), 28, 29 (all), 31, 32, 34, 36 (bottom), 41, 55 (top left), 57 (left); Museum of the City of New York/Corbis, 10; Corbis, 13, 19, 46, 55 (bottom left); New Hampshire Historical Society, 16; Library of Congress, 30, 58 (right); Bettmann/Corbis, 35, 40, 59 (left); Naval Historical Center, 42; David J. and Janice L. Frent Collection/Corbis, 43; University of Rochester Library, Rare Books and Special Collections, 55 (right); Texas State Library and Archives Commission, 56 (right).

Editors: E. Russell Primm, Emily J. Dolbear, Melissa McDaniel, and Catherine Neitge
Photo Researcher: Svetlana Zhurkina
Photo Selector: Linda S. Koutris
Designer: The Design Lab
Cartographer: XNR Productions, Inc.

Library of Congress Cataloging-in-Publication Data

Somervill, Barbara A.
 Franklin Pierce / by Barbara Somervill.
  p. cm. — (Profiles of the presidents)
Includes bibliographical references and index.
 ISBN 0-7565-0262-4
 1. Pierce, Franklin, 1804–1869—Juvenile literature. 2. Presidents—United States—Biography—Juvenile literature. 3. United States—Politics and government—1853–1857—Juvenile literature. [1. Pierce, Franklin, 1804–1869. 2. Presidents.] I. Title. II. Series.
 E432.S66 S66 2002
 973.6'6'092—dc21   2002003014

Printed in the United States of America.

Table of Contents

★ ★ ★

Franklin Who?

★　★　★

In 1852, the Democratic Party met to choose a **candidate** for president of the United States. Four men wanted the job: James Buchanan, Lewis Cass, William Marcy, and Stephen A. Douglas. Each man represented a powerful group, but none had enough support to be **nominated.** After thirty-four votes with no winner, the Democrats looked for a new candidate. They chose Franklin Pierce.

On the forty-ninth vote, Pierce became the candidate. His wife, Jane, fainted when she learned her husband had

Although unknown throughout much of the country, Franklin Pierce became the fourteenth U.S. president.

agreed to run.
Though he was a
favorite in his
home state of New
Hampshire and
well-known within
his party, he was
not a national figure.
The Whigs, the
other major United
States political party
at the time, asked,
"Who's Frank
Pierce?"

Lewis Cass was the
Democratic presidential
candidate in 1848,
but lost the election
to Zachary Taylor. He
also wanted to run
in 1852.

Pierce was handsome, charming, a good speaker,
and a former officer in the U.S. Army. He also supported the right of the southern states to maintain slavery.
This made him popular in the South, where slavery was
legal. But it upset many people in the North, where
slavery had been outlawed.

The Whigs nominated General Winfield Scott, who
gave a few long, boring speeches during the campaign.
Franklin Pierce won the election, ending what one news-

General Winfield ▶
Scott, the Whig
Party candidate

paper said was the most "uninteresting presidential campaign" ever.

Pierce was not ready for the job of president. The United States was facing a crisis over the issue of slavery. Few men would have been up to the challenge of keeping the North and South from drifting apart. A 1992 poll of history professors ranked Pierce as one of the five worst United States presidents ever to hold office.

Student, Lawyer, Politician

★ ★ ★

On November 23, 1804, Franklin Pierce was born
to Benjamin and Anna Pierce in Hillsborough, New
Hampshire. Franklin was one of eight children. The
family lived in a log cabin on a 50-acre (120-hectare)
farm. The children
shared farm chores,
hunted, fished, and
played in the woods
near their home.

▾ *Benjamin Pierce*

Their father,
Benjamin Pierce, had
been eighteen when the
Revolutionary War
(1775–1783) started. He
picked up his gun and
powder horn and joined

9

the other **colonists** in their fight for independence from Great Britain. Benjamin was an excellent soldier who rose through the ranks to become an army officer. He did so well that General George Washington named him a "valuable" military leader.

George Washington, ▲
Revolutionary War
general and the first
U.S. president

After the war, Benjamin Pierce settled in Hillsborough, where he ran his farm and served on the city council. When New Hampshire set up a **militia,** Benjamin Pierce became its brigadier general. Later, Benjamin Pierce served two terms as New Hampshire's governor. For young Franklin, his father's military and public service set an example he hoped to follow in later life.

By age eleven, Franklin's schooling at Hillsborough's brick schoolhouse came to an end. After that, his parents sent him to three different boarding schools to prepare him for college.

In 1820, at only sixteen years old, Franklin headed to Bowdoin College in Maine. There he studied the usual subjects of the time: Greek, Latin, and mathematics. He joined clubs and enjoyed himself so much that his grades suffered. By the end of his second year, Franklin ranked last in his class. He knew he needed to get serious about school. Young Pierce then began to study hard. By the time he graduated in 1824, he was near the top of his class.

College life gave Franklin Pierce valuable experience. During his stay at Bowdoin, he became captain

◄ *Franklin Pierce enjoyed life at Bowdoin College in Maine.*

Nathaniel Hawthorne ▶

of the student military company. Like his father before him, Franklin enjoyed military life and seemed to be an able leader. At college, he also became friends with Nathaniel Hawthorne.

Hawthorne later wrote the famous novels *The Scarlet Letter* and *The House of the Seven Gables,* as well as Pierce's biography.

After college, Pierce decided to become a lawyer. He first studied law under Governor Levi Woodbury, a former judge. The Woodbury and Pierce families were friends. Benjamin Pierce had been influential in Levi Woodbury being named a judge.

From Governor Woodbury's offices, Pierce left for law school in Northampton, Massachusetts. In 1827, Pierce opened his own law office in Concord, New

◄ *Franklin Pierce's law offices in Concord, New Hampshire*

Hampshire. He soon handled his first court case—and lost. When another lawyer offered words of comfort, Pierce replied, "I will try nine hundred and ninety-nine cases if clients will continue to trust me, and if I fail just as I have today, will try the thousandth."

During that year, Pierce's father was elected governor of New Hampshire. Benjamin Pierce thought Franklin was an excellent public speaker and believed that the young man should enter politics. Only two years later, at age twenty-four, Franklin Pierce was elected to New Hampshire's **legislature.**

The Pierces belonged to the Democratic Party, the party in power in New Hampshire and in the federal government. Before he turned thirty, Franklin Pierce was elected to the U.S. House of Representatives. He was the ideal Democrat—and almost always voted according to the party's wishes.

For Pierce, Washington life seemed dull. Thorough-

Though Pierce found them unexciting, debates in the House of Representatives could be quite lively.

ly bored, he attended many
social events. Although he
was normally pleasant,
Pierce often drank too
much alcohol at these
events and became
gossipy and wild.
Later in life, Pierce's
drinking would
become a serious
problem.

▲ *Jane Pierce*

In 1834, Franklin
Pierce married Jane Means
Appleton. Although Jane was not
well suited to being a politician's wife, Pierce loved her
very much. She was very shy and she was in poor
health. Also, she had no interest in politics or the social
events that went along with it. In 1836, Jane Pierce gave
birth to their first child, Franklin Jr. Sadly, the baby
died within three days. Jane was heartbroken.

At this time, Franklin Pierce was still a member of the
House of Representatives. He voted against any bill that
spent tax money, regardless of the need. For example, he

Jane Pierce with
Benjamin, her
third son

opposed building new roads, canals, or harbors, although the growing United States needed better transportation. He simply did not think the federal government should deal with those issues.

Pierce remained popular among Democrats because he followed their policies to the letter. The party rewarded Pierce by choosing him to represent New Hampshire in the U.S. Senate beginning in 1837.

Between December 1838 and August 1839, family events took over Franklin and Jane Pierce's lives. Both of Franklin's parents died. Then Franklin and Jane's second son, Frank Robert, was born. This child thrived, but Jane Pierce's health faded. Yet within two years, she was expecting their third child. Benjamin Pierce, named for his grandfather, arrived in April 1841. In early 1842, Franklin Pierce quit the Senate to live in New Hampshire and care for Jane. Even an offer to be in President James Polk's **cabinet** could not tempt him back to Washington, D.C. But the Pierces could not seem to find peace. At age four, their second son, Frank, died of typhoid fever.

James Polk was president from 1845 to 1849.

In New Hampshire, Pierce began speaking out against drinking alcohol, even though in the past he himself drank too much. But he was politically active only in New Hampshire.

A War and an Election

★ ★ ★

In 1846, the United States was at war against Mexico. The United States had tried to add land in California and New Mexico to the nation. Mexico owned this land and was not willing to part with it. Then, in 1845, the United States added Texas as a state. Mexico still claimed Texas, though. Mexico and the United States didn't agree where the borders were. So President James Polk sent in troops.

The Battle of Buena ▶ Vista ended the war in northern Mexico.

The Mexican army faced the American troops across the Rio Grande. The United States was once again at war.

In the military, few people rose as fast as Franklin Pierce did. At the beginning of the war, he helped sign up men from New Hampshire for the army. Pierce himself entered the army as a private in 1846. By February

▲ *Brigadier General Franklin Pierce*

1847, President Polk had made Pierce a colonel. Three weeks later, Pierce became a brigadier general in charge of 2,000 troops. His rapid rise in rank, however, did not mean that Pierce was a successful officer. In fact, errors and accidents blotted his army record.

Pierce and his men arrived in Veracruz, Mexico, expecting to meet General Winfield Scott's army. But Scott had already moved on to Puebla, 150 miles (240 kilometers) away. Pierce planned to leave for Puebla to join Scott, using

General Pierce ▶
landing in Mexico

mules to pull the supply wagons. In his journal, he described the first problem with this: "About two thousand wild mules had been collected; but . . . a stampede has occurred to-day, by which fifteen hundred have been lost."

In addition, Pierce's troops were poorly prepared for the Mexican summer. Their wool uniforms were much too hot for the high temperatures. Many men also became sick with yellow fever and diarrhea.

The men caught wild mules and horses every day to prepare for the trip to Puebla. But the animals had to get used to wearing a bridle and harness before they could pull wagons. Finally, after three weeks, Pierce's troops set out for Puebla. The brigade's progress was slow and difficult. Pierce wrote in his journal, "The road was very heavy; the wheels sinking almost to the hubs in sand, and the untried and untamed teams almost constantly bolting. . . . At ten o'clock at night, we [camped] in the darkness and sand, by the wagons in the road, having made but three miles from camp."

The march from Veracruz to Puebla moved at a snail's pace. In many places, there were no real roads. The men often had to build bridges to carry the wagons over rivers. And sometimes small groups of Mexican soldiers attacked. These attacks cost few lives, but they slowed down Pierce even further. Pierce and his men had been in Mexico more than a month before they were able to join General Scott's army at Puebla.

The Mexican War (1846–1848) cost the United States at least 12,000 lives, though fewer than 1,800 deaths resulted from battle.

Pierce's first real battle took place on August 18, 1847. Early in the fight, Pierce's horse stumbled. It fell on Pierce's leg, wrenching his knee. Overcome with pain,

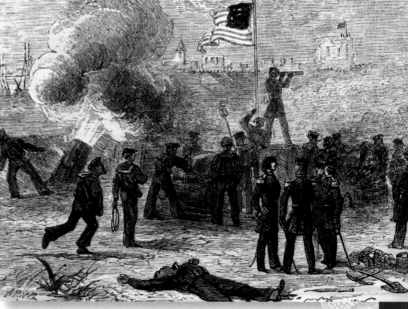

Pierce fainted. His political opponents would later call him "Fainting Frank."

The next clash took place at Molino del Rey. Pierce, still suffering from his knee injury, took charge of the reserve troops. These soldiers were supposed to help the main troops when needed. The battle ended quickly, though, and Pierce's troops never saw any fighting.

When he was finally fit enough to lead again, Pierce looked forward to the Battle of Chapultepec. He hoped to finally win some glory for himself as an officer. Unfortunately, he came down with a bad case of diarrhea. He left his sickbed to lead his troops. But the Mexican army gave up before he and his men reached the battle. The Mexican War ended, and with it, Franklin Pierce's hopes of military glory.

Victory in the Mexican War added the land that would become California, Nevada, Utah, and parts of Wyoming, Colorado, Arizona, and New Mexico to the United States. Great Britain had already given up its claims to Washington, Oregon, Idaho, and part of Wyoming. The United States was now almost as big as Europe!

With this new land came bitter arguments between

northerners and southerners. They argued over whether new states or territories should allow slavery. As the 1852 presidential election drew near, the Democratic Party was desperate. Northern and southern Democrats could not agree on a candidate. After forty-nine votes, the Democrats finally settled on Franklin Pierce, a northerner who favored slavery.

Pierce's commander from the Mexican War, General Winfield Scott, ran as the Whig candidate. A third man, John P. Hale, was the candidate of the Free Soil Party. But the race was really between Fainting Frank and Old

▾ The United States after its post-war treaty with Mexico

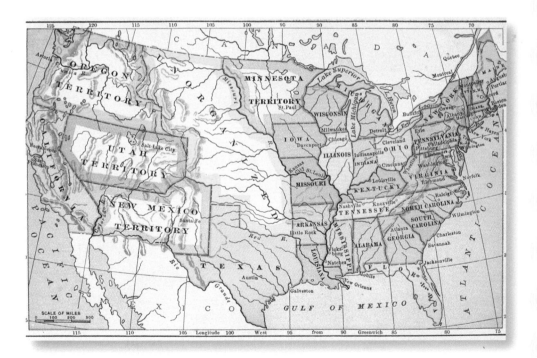

The United States had been divided over the issue of slavery since the early days of its history.

John P. Hale

Fuss and Feathers—as dull, stiff General Winfield Scott was sometimes called. Southern voters were angered by his stand against slavery. He lost the election, and Franklin Pierce became the fourteenth president of the United States.

Between the presidential election and the day Franklin Pierce took office, tragedy struck his family once again. The Pierces were in a terrible train accident. Their third and only living child,

Benjamin, was killed.
Although Jane Pierce was
unhurt, she never recov-
ered from the accident.
She lived like a ghost in
the White House, hiding
from public view and
haunted by her loss.

Pierce himself was
little better. He mourned his son and paid little atten-
tion to his job. His presidency seemed cursed from the
beginning. Vice President William Rufus King took the
oath of office from his sickbed in Cuba and died six
weeks later. Pierce would serve his four-year term with-

▲ *Inauguration Day
parade for
President Franklin
Pierce*

▲ *William Rufus King*

out a vice president. Pierce's first job as president was to form a cabinet. He tried to balance southerners and northerners in an effort to keep all parts of the Democratic Party happy. Unfortunately, many Democrats did not like his choices, and Pierce found it hard to get his cabinet members approved by Congress.

Secretary of State ▶
William Marcy

Pierce's presidential cabinet is the only one in which every member served all four years. Northerner William Marcy became secretary of state, the person in charge of dealing with foreign countries. Another northerner, James Campbell, served as postmaster general, while Robert McClelland became secretary of the interior. From the South, Pierce named James Guthrie secretary of the treasury and James Dobbin secretary of the navy. Caleb Cushing—a Whig rather than a Democrat—served as attorney general, the nation's top lawyer.

The most famous member of Pierce's cabinet was Jefferson Davis, the secretary of war. Davis later became the president of the Confederacy, the government of the Southern states that left the Union during the Civil War (1861-1865). As secretary of war, Davis tried to strengthen the U.S. Army. Strangely, his efforts came back to haunt him, when the more powerful Union army defeated his Confederate army in the Civil War.

◄ *Attorney General Caleb Cushing*

◄ *Secretary of War Jefferson Davis*

Problems Across the Country

★　★　★

When Pierce became president, the United States was growing and changing. The nation had recently gained more land by adding the Oregon Territory and the lands

Building a ▶
coast-to-coast
railroad involved
digging deep
tunnels, building
bridges, and laying
thousands of miles
of track.

won in the Mexican War. At the same time, the California gold rush drew miners to the West. Railroad lines connected Chicago, Illinois, to cities along the East Coast for the first time, while railroad companies were laying tracks to join the East and West Coasts.

Manufacturing was becoming an increasingly important part of the nation's economy. In many northern cities, bustling factories turned out cloth, tools, and household goods. In Pittsburgh, the first oil refinery in the United States opened in 1858.

Throughout the 1850s, Americans were amazed by new inventions, including Singer's sewing machine, Page's electric locomotive, Otis's elevator, and Gail Borden's process for making condensed milk. A startling new idea in 1856 was H. L. Lipman's pencil with an eraser attached.

Across the country, people enjoyed poetry by Henry

▲ *Manufacturing revolutionized American life in the 1850s with the growth of the factory workforce (left) and new inventions, such as the sewing machine (right).*

Wadsworth Longfellow, John Greenleaf Whittier, and Walt Whitman. They read Herman Melville's novel *Moby Dick*, and Harriet Beecher Stowe's *Uncle Tom's Cabin*. People sang such songs as "Jeannie with the Light-Brown Hair" and "My Old Kentucky Home." In sports, 1857 would see the first national baseball league formed. It had twenty-five clubs.

Harriet Beecher Stowe ▶

With America doing well, it might seem that Pierce would have had an easy four years in office. But he faced problems he could not solve. The most serious problem was the growing anger between the **pro-slavery** South and the **antislavery** North.

In 1853, the United States bought land in what is

now southern Arizona and New Mexico from the Mexican government for $10 million. This land provided a southern route for a railroad connecting California with the East. James Gadsden, the U.S. representative to Mexico, had arranged the sale. Pierce thought the Gadsden Purchase made sense, but other politicians threatened to block the deal unless he agreed to sign the Kansas–Nebraska Act of 1854. Foolishly, Pierce gave in, and the Kansas–Nebraska Act became law. This law would turn out to be Pierce's downfall.

Earlier in the 1800s, Congress had passed two major agreements about expanding slavery. They were

▲ The Gadsden Purchase added the territory that now forms parts of southern Arizona and New Mexico.

the Missouri Compromise of 1820 and the Compromise of 1850. The first said that slavery would not be allowed in territories above 36°30' north latitude. This line lay along the southern border of Missouri. The second agreement, the Compromise of 1850, had several different parts. First, the United States admitted California as a Free State, while forming the New Mexico and Utah Territories without mention of slavery.

Stephen A. ▼
Douglas

The Compromise of 1850 also ended the slave trade in Washington, D.C., and put a stronger runaway-slave law into action.

President Pierce thought the slavery issue had been settled, but he was wrong. In 1854, Senator Stephen A. Douglas of Illinois introduced the Kansas–Nebraska

Act in the U.S. Senate. The proposed law would let voters in Kansas and Nebraska decide for themselves whether to allow slavery in their territories. The bill barely passed in the Senate and the House of Representatives. Then it went to Pierce, who signed it into law.

◄ *Andrew Reeder*

Trouble began immediately. Pierce named Andrew Reeder, a northerner, as governor of Kansas Territory. Reeder, who made a living buying cheap land and selling it at a higher price, did not have the skills needed to govern the territory.

Kansas held an election to choose the members of the territorial legislature. Although only 2,905 voters were listed in Kansas, more than 6,300 votes were

Settlers moved ▶ from Missouri into Kansas to vote in pro-slavery elections.

counted. Pro-slavery settlers from Missouri had simply crossed the border and voted illegally. Anger raged over the illegal election, but President Pierce accepted the result. Kansas's new pro-slavery legislature went to work in the town of Shawnee.

Within a year, antislavery settlers in Kansas had voted in a new governor and legislature, located in Topeka. This meant that two different governments were trying to run the same territory. Soon a civil war spread across the new territory. The war became known as Bleeding Kansas. Pierce tried to convince Congress to send in troops. Southerners, however, were so angry over his choosing Reeder as governor that they would not support his efforts. So Pierce fired Reeder, which angered northerners. Meanwhile, Kansas's pro-slavery and antislavery groups continued their bitter fight. By late 1856, more than 200 people had been killed.

▼ *Kansas went to war over slavery years before the nation entered the Civil War.*

Finally, Pierce named another man, John White Geary, governor of Kansas and backed him up with federal troops. An uneasy peace settled over the territory.

Besides the Kansas–Nebraska disaster, Pierce also faced growing concern over

John White ▲
Geary

Immigrants ▶
landing in
New York

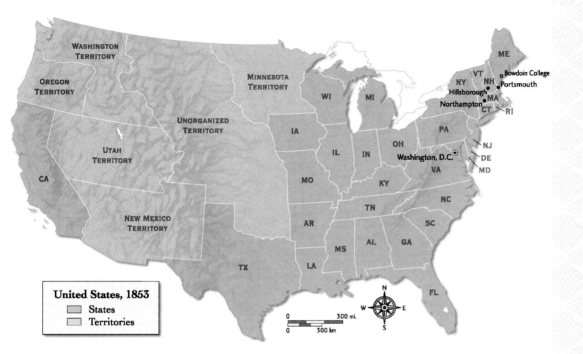

United States, 1853
- States
- Territories

the large number of **immigrants** arriving in the United States. Irish and eastern European immigrants flooded into Boston and New York City. More than 13,000 Chinese immigrants entered California. Many of these immigrants worked for low wages. This angered some U.S. citizens who felt they were losing jobs to immigrants who would work for less. Pierce believed that immigrants should be granted the same legal rights as U.S. citizens. This view was very unpopular.

Dealing with Foreign Countries

★ ★ ★

Pierce had almost as little success dealing with foreign countries as he did at home. In most cases, his efforts showed poor planning and lack of common sense. From the beginning, Pierce thought other nations would fall into line with his plans, but they did not.

Matthew Perry meets successfully with the Japanese. ▼

One effort that did succeed involved Japan. In 1853, Commodore Matthew Perry of the U.S. Navy

arrived in Yedo Bay, Japan. Up to this point, Japan had kept to itself and did not trade with other countries. Perry asked Japan to open its doors to trade with the United States. Japan agreed several months later. While Perry's trip was successful, it was Millard Fillmore, the president before Pierce, who ordered it. Credit for the idea and results usually goes to Fillmore.

◀ *Millard Fillmore,*
the thirteenth
president of the
United States

Pierce's inexperience in dealing with other countries sometimes created problems. In one case, Great Britain and the United States were arguing over who was allowed to fish off the Canadian coast. The two nations had just reached an agreement when Pierce learned that the British **ambassador** was signing up Americans to fight in Britain's war against Russia. Pierce was outraged. He sent the ambassador back to England, making the British furious.

Another Pierce political disaster dealt with the Central American country of Nicaragua. An American named William Walker took over Nicaragua and set himself up as its president.

William Walker ▶

Walker wanted to begin farming in Nicaragua, using slaves. He hoped that in time the country would become a U.S.

state. Walker's plans did not suit Cornelius Vanderbilt, a wealthy American railroad owner who wanted to build rail lines through Nicaragua. Vanderbilt talked Pierce into sending the U.S. Navy to force Walker to give

◄ *Cornelius Vanderbilt*

up. Walker fled to Honduras, where he was caught by the British navy and killed by a firing squad. Many politicians felt that Pierce had no right to send the U.S. Navy to Nicaragua, and they said so.

Even less successful was Pierce's plan to buy Cuba from Spain. Some southerners wanted to add Cuba, an island off the Florida coast, to the United States because slavery was strong there.

Pierce sent Pierre Soulé, a southern landowner, to Spain to discuss the idea. Soulé could offer up to $150 million for Cuba. He tried to bully the Spanish king into selling. The more Soulé threatened, the less likely the king was to sell.

John Mason ▶

Finally, Soulé called a meeting in Ostend, Belgium, with James Buchanan, the U.S. representative in England, and John Mason, the U.S. representative in France. The three created the Ostend **Manifesto.** Under this plan, the United States threatened to attack Spain if it did not agree to sell Cuba. When other European countries heard about the Ostend Manifesto, they were outraged. The Ostend Manifesto disappeared quickly, along with any hope that the United States might buy Cuba.

In the Shadows

★ ★ ★

Major political changes took place while Pierce was president. Northern Democrats and Whigs, angry over the Kansas–Nebraska Act and Bleeding Kansas, formed a new party—the Republican Party. The Republicans opposed slavery. They supported using taxes to protect American businesses and wanted a railroad built across the country. Another new political party, the Native Americans, or Know-Nothing Party, was against giving immigrants legal rights.

When Pierce took office, the Democratic Party controlled the United States Senate and House of

◄ The Know-Nothing Party used anti-immigrant slogans in its campaigns.

Representatives. The 1853 Senate had thirty-eight Democrats, twenty-two Whigs, and two Free Soilers. That same year, the House of Representatives had one hundred fifty-nine Democrats, seventy-one Whigs, and four members from other parties.

After the 1854 elections, the Senate showed little change, but power shifted in the House of Representatives. The Whig Party all but disappeared. The brand-new Republican Party gained control in the House of Representatives with one hundred eight representatives to the Democrats' eighty-three. Whigs, Free Soilers, and Know-Nothings held forty-three seats. President Pierce would find it difficult to get any new laws passed by the House of Representatives.

When the Democrats met to choose their candidate for the 1856 presidential election, Franklin Pierce wanted to be nominated. He was so unpopular, however, that the Democrats would not risk letting him run again. Instead, James Buchanan became

James Buchanan was nominated by the Democrats as the 1856 presidential candidate instead of Franklin Pierce.

the Democratic candidate. He won the election and became the fifteenth U.S. president.

Immediately after leaving the White House, Franklin and Jane Pierce went to Europe for a long vacation. Jane had never regained her health after losing her son Benjamin. The pair stayed on Madeira, a Portuguese island in the

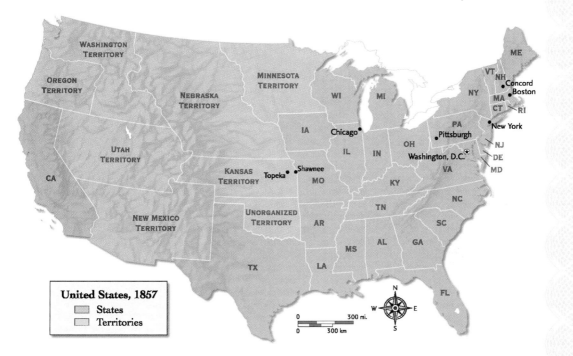

United States, 1857
- States
- Territories

Atlantic Ocean. They spent three years in Europe before returning to Concord, New Hampshire, in 1860.

The harbor on ▼
Madeira, where the
Pierces spent some
time after they left
the White House

By that time, the North–South split that had caused Bleeding Kansas threatened the entire country. In November, Republican Abraham Lincoln was elected

president. Within weeks, Southern states began withdraw-
ing from the Union.

Pierce was asked to step in and heal the break
between North and South, but he refused. Pierce
believed that the Southern states had the right to leave

◀ *Abraham Lincoln, the
sixteenth president
of the United States,
was elected in 1860.*

the Union. He also believed that slavery was legal. These beliefs gained Pierce friends in the South, but his fellow Northerners called him a traitor. Lincoln's secretary of state, William Seward, openly accused Pierce of **treason** against the Union.

In April 1861, the Civil War began. Pierce supported the Union, but he still thought that the Southern states had the right to govern themselves.

In 1863, Jane Pierce died of tuberculosis, a disease of the lungs. Alone, Franklin Pierce again began drinking too much. He lived like a hermit, rarely going out in public. He never again worked as a lawyer, and he stayed away from politics.

When Abraham Lincoln was shot and killed in 1865,

William Seward ▼

Northern tempers raged. Across the North, citizens flew American flags to show their love of country and sadness over Lincoln's death. In Concord, people marched to Pierce's home, asking why the former president did not fly the flag. Pierce said, "If the period which I have served our state and country . . . has left in doubt the question of my devotion to the flag, the Constitution, and the Union, it is too late to rescue it by any such exhibition."

▼ *President Lincoln's funeral in April 1865*

THE NATION MOURNS.

Franklin Pierce died on October 8, 1869, of a liver disease brought on by his heavy drinking. He is remembered as a weak president whose one major act helped bring about the Civil War. This may or may not be fair. It is true that many of his actions as president were unpopular and ended poorly. Still, it should be remembered that he did what he thought was best to preserve the Union. It was his greatest sorrow to know he had failed his country.

GLOSSARY

★ ★ ★

ambassador—the representative of a nation's government in another country

antislavery—against allowing people to own slaves

cabinet—a president's group of advisers

candidate—someone running for office in an election

colonists—people living in a newly settled area

immigrants—people who move from one country to live permanently in another

legislature—the part of government that makes or changes laws

manifesto—an official notice

militia—an army of part-time soldiers

nominated—chosen to run as a candidate in an election

powder horn—container that holds gunpowder

pro-slavery—in favor of allowing people to own slaves

treason—an attempt to betray one's own country

FRANKLIN PIERCE'S LIFE AT A GLANCE

★ ★ ★

PERSONAL

Nickname:	Young Hickory of the Granite Hills
Birth date:	November 23, 1804
Birthplace:	Hillsborough (now Hillsboro), New Hampshire
Father's name:	Benjamin Pierce
Mother's name:	Anna Kendrick Pierce
Education:	Graduated from Bowdoin College in 1824
Wife's name:	Jane Means Appleton Pierce
Married:	November 10, 1834
Children:	Franklin Pierce (1836); Frank Robert Pierce (1839–1843); Benjamin Pierce (1841–1853)
Died:	October 8, 1869, in Concord, New Hampshire
Buried:	Old North Cemetery in Concord, New Hampshire

PUBLIC

Occupation before presidency:	Lawyer, public official
Occupation after presidency:	Retired
Military service:	Brigadier general in the U.S. Army during the Mexican War
Other government positions:	Member of the New Hampshire House of Representatives; member of the U.S. House of Representatives from New Hampshire; U.S. senator from New Hampshire
Political party:	Democrat
Vice president:	William R. King (1853)
Dates in office:	March 4, 1853–March 3, 1857
Presidential opponent:	Winfield Scott (Whig), 1852
Number of votes (Electoral College):	1,607,510 of 2,994,452 (254 of 296)
Writings:	None

Franklin Pierce's Cabinet

Secretary of state:
William L. Marcy (1853–1857)

Secretary of the treasury:
James Guthrie (1853–1857)

Secretary of war:
Jefferson Davis (1853–1857)

Attorney general:
Caleb Cushing (1853–1857)

Postmaster general:
James Campbell (1853–1857)

Secretary of the navy:
James C. Dobbin (1853–1857)

Secretary of the interior:
Robert McClelland (1853–1857)

FRANKLIN PIERCE'S LIFE AND TIMES

★ ★ ★

PIERCE'S LIFE

November 23, Franklin Pierce (above) is born in Hillsborough, New Hampshire

1804

WORLD EVENTS

1799   Napoléon Bonaparte (below) takes control of France

1800

1801   German scientist Johann Ritter discovers ultraviolet radiation

1805   Japanese doctor Hanaoka Seishu uses general anesthesia in surgery for the first time

1809   American poet and short-story writer Edgar Allen Poe is born in Boston

PIERCE'S LIFE

WORLD EVENTS

1810

1810   Chile fights for its independence from Spain

1812–
1814   The United States and Britain fight the War of 1812

1820

1820   Susan B. Anthony, (right) a leader of the American woman suffrage movement, is born

Graduates from Bowdoin College (above)   1824

1823   Mexico becomes a republic

1826   The first photograph is taken by Joseph Niépce, a French physicist

Begins practicing law in New Hampshire (above)   1827

1827   Modern-day matches are invented by coating the end of a wooden stick with phosphorus

Is elected to the New Hampshire House of Representatives   1829

1829   The first practical sewing machine is invented by French tailor Barthélemy Thimonnier

PIERCE'S LIFE		WORLD EVENTS

1830

Serves as speaker of the New Hampshire House of Representatives — 1831

Is elected to the U.S. House of Representatives — 1833

1833 — Great Britain abolishes slavery

November 19, marries Jane Appleton (below) — 1834

1836 — Texans defeat Mexican troops at San Jacinto after a deadly battle at the Alamo (above)

Becomes a U.S. senator from New Hampshire — 1837

1837 — American banker J. P. Morgan is born

PIERCE'S LIFE

WORLD EVENTS

1840

1840   Auguste Rodin, famous sculptor of *The Thinker,* is born

Resigns from the   1842
Senate

Is appointed New   1845
Hampshire federal
district attorney

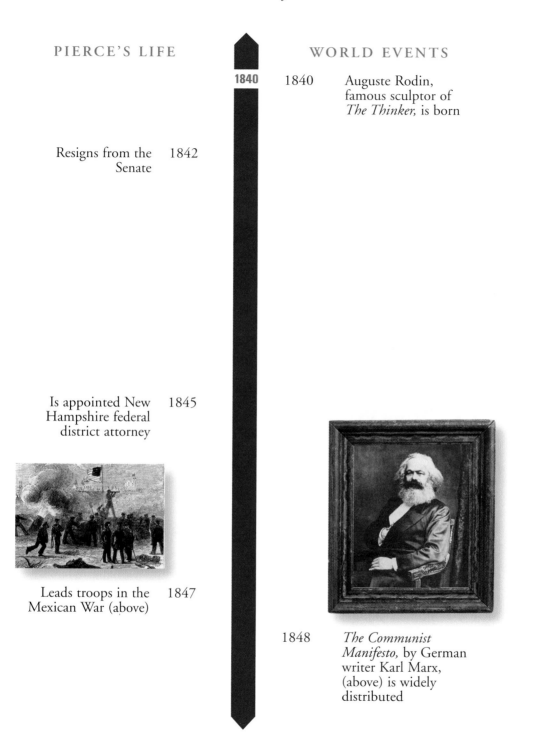

Leads troops in the   1847
Mexican War (above)

1848   *The Communist Manifesto,* by German writer Karl Marx, (above) is widely distributed

PIERCE'S LIFE

1850

WORLD EVENTS

January 6, the Pierces are in a train wreck, which kills their son — 1853

1852 American Harriet Beecher Stowe (below) publishes *Uncle Tom's Cabin*

The United States adds part of New Mexico and Arizona in the Gadsden Purchase

Presidential Election Results:		Popular Votes	Electoral Votes
1852	Franklin Pierce	1,607,510	254
	Winfield Scott	1,386,942	42

The Kansas–Nebraska Act becomes law, allowing voters in the two territories to decide the slavery issue. Soon Kansas and Nebraska are war zones. — 1854

The U.S. and Japan sign a treaty opening up trade between the nations (below)

PIERCE'S LIFE

1854 Pierce's advisers write the Ostend Manifesto, which says that the United States has the right to seize Cuba from Spain

1856 Violence erupts between pro-slavery and antislavery forces in what is known as Bleeding Kansas (below)

1863 Jane Pierce dies of tuberculosis

1869 October 8, dies in Concord, New Hampshire

WORLD EVENTS

1858 English scientist Charles Darwin (above) presents his theory of evolution

1860 Austrian composer Gustav Mahler is born in Kalischt (now in Austria)

1865 *Tristan and Isolde,* by German composer Richard Wagner, opens in Munich

1868 Louisa May Alcott publishes *Little Women*

1869 The periodic table of elements is invented

The transcontinental railroad across the United States is completed

1860

UNDERSTANDING FRANKLIN PIERCE AND HIS PRESIDENCY

★ ★ ★

IN THE LIBRARY

Ferry, Steven. *Franklin Pierce.* Chanhassen, Minn.:
The Child's World, 2002.

Simon, Charnan. *Franklin Pierce.* Chicago:
Childrens Press, 1988.

Welsbacher, Anne. *Franklin Pierce.* Minneapolis:
Abdo & Daughters, 2001.

ON THE WEB

Franklin Pierce
http://www.whitehouse.gov/history/presidents/fp14.html
To learn more about Pierce's life and presidency

Internet Public Library—Franklin Pierce
http://www.ipl.org/ref/POTUS/fpierce.html
For information and links about Pierce's administration and life

Pierce Manse
http://www.newww.com/free/pierce/pierce.html
To read about Pierce's home, which is now a national historic site

Pierce's Inaugural Address
http://www.newww.com/free/pierce/pierce.html
To read the full text of Pierce's inaugural address

Pierce's Obituary
http://starship.python.net/crew/manus/Presidents/fp/fpobit.html
To read the *New York Times* obituary of the president

The American President—Franklin Pierce
http://www.americanpresident.org/KoTrain/Courses/FP/FP_In_Brief.htm
For information and many links about Pierce and his presidency

PIERCE HISTORIC SITES
ACROSS THE COUNTRY

The Pierce Manse
14 Penacook Street
Concord, NH 00301
603/224-7668
To tour the Pierce family home

The Pierce Homestead
Routes 9 and 31
Hillsboro, NH 03244
603/478-3913
To tour Pierce's childhood home

THE U.S. PRESIDENTS
(Years in Office)

★　★　★

1. **George Washington**
   (March 4, 1789–March 3, 1797)
2. **John Adams**
   (March 4, 1797–March 3, 1801)
3. **Thomas Jefferson**
   (March 4, 1801–March 3, 1809)
4. **James Madison**
   (March 4, 1809–March 3, 1817)
5. **James Monroe**
   (March 4, 1817–March 3, 1825)
6. **John Quincy Adams**
   (March 4, 1825–March 3, 1829)
7. **Andrew Jackson**
   (March 4, 1829–March 3, 1837)
8. **Martin Van Buren**
   (March 4, 1837–March 3, 1841)
9. **William Henry Harrison**
   (March 6, 1841–April 4, 1841)
10. **John Tyler**
    (April 6, 1841–March 3, 1845)
11. **James K. Polk**
    (March 4, 1845–March 3, 1849)
12. **Zachary Taylor**
    (March 5, 1849–July 9, 1850)
13. **Millard Fillmore**
    (July 10, 1850–March 3, 1853)
14. Franklin Pierce
    (March 4, 1853–March 3, 1857)
15. **James Buchanan**
    (March 4, 1857–March 3, 1861)
16. **Abraham Lincoln**
    (March 4, 1861–April 15, 1865)
17. **Andrew Johnson**
    (April 15, 1865–March 3, 1869)

18. **Ulysses S. Grant**
    (March 4, 1869–March 3, 1877)
19. **Rutherford B. Hayes**
    (March 4, 1877–March 3, 1881)
20. **James Garfield**
    (March 4, 1881–Sept 19, 1881)
21. **Chester Arthur**
    (Sept 20, 1881–March 3, 1885)
22. **Grover Cleveland**
    (March 4, 1885–March 3, 1889)
23. **Benjamin Harrison**
    (March 4, 1889–March 3, 1893)
24. **Grover Cleveland**
    (March 4, 1893–March 3, 1897)
25. **William McKinley**
    (March 4, 1897–
    September 14, 1901)
26. **Theodore Roosevelt**
    (September 14, 1901–
    March 3, 1909)
27. **William Howard Taft**
    (March 4, 1909–March 3, 1913)
28. **Woodrow Wilson**
    (March 4, 1913–March 3, 1921)
29. **Warren G. Harding**
    (March 4, 1921–August 2, 1923)
30. **Calvin Coolidge**
    (August 3, 1923–March 3, 1929)
31. **Herbert Hoover**
    (March 4, 1929–March 3, 1933)
32. **Franklin D. Roosevelt**
    (March 4, 1933–April 12, 1945)

33. **Harry S. Truman**
    (April 12, 1945–
    January 20, 1953)
34. **Dwight D. Eisenhower**
    (January 20, 1953–
    January 20, 1961)
35. **John F. Kennedy**
    (January 20, 1961–
    November 22, 1963)
36. **Lyndon B. Johnson**
    (November 22, 1963–
    January 20, 1969)
37. **Richard M. Nixon**
    (January 20, 1969–
    August 9, 1974)
38. **Gerald R. Ford**
    (August 9, 1974–
    January 20, 1977)
39. **James Earl Carter**
    (January 20, 1977–
    January 20, 1981)
40. **Ronald Reagan**
    (January 20, 1981–
    January 20, 1989)
41. **George H. W. Bush**
    (January 20, 1989–
    January 20, 1993)
42. **William Jefferson Clinton**
    (January 20, 1993–
    January 20, 2001)
43. **George W. Bush**
    (January 20, 2001–)

INDEX

★ ★ ★

Index

ABOUT THE AUTHOR

Barbara Somervill is a lifelong learner. Every project she undertakes provides her an opportunity to learn new information, understand a historical period, or develop an appreciation for life in other times.

She writes books, video scripts, magazine articles, and textbooks. One of her strangest subjects was a script about coffins!

Somervill grew up and went to school in New York. She received a bachelor's degree in English and a master's degree in education. She lives in South Carolina and is an avid reader and traveler, and enjoys movies and theater.